The Comma After Love

Akron Series in Poetry

The Comma After Love

Selected Poems of Raeburn Miller

Edited by Donald Justice,
Cooper R. Mackin,
and Richard D. Olson

With an Introduction by
Donald Justice

The University of Akron Press
Akron, Ohio

Many of these poems were first published in the literary magazines and annuals acknowledged below. Every effort has been made to secure the copyright or permission to reprint.

A Book of the Year, 1962 (Poetry Society of Texas): "On Millay's Translation of Baudelaire"; *A Houyhnhnm's Scrapbook:* "Letter Found in a Refrigerator"; *Austin Poetry Society Yearbook:* "In Memory of an Actor," "Rationale of Dissipation"; *Bogg:* "A Curse from Propertius"; *The Carleton Miscellany:* "Two Fragments Toward a Suicide Note"; *The Daily Iowan:* "The Right Choice"; *Ellipsis:* "Ahasuerus," "Dispositions," "Peptides," "Poets and Their Bibliographies"; *Epos:* "Convertible Invocations"; *Fiddlehead:* "Poem Instead of a Letter"; *Illinois Quarterly:* "For a Saint"; *Integrity: "Luxe, Calme"*; *International Literary Annual 2:* "Prose Poems (Group I)"; *The Kansas City Star:* "Scraps"; *The MacGuffin:* "Gulf Breeze"; *Maple Leaf Rag: An Anthology of New Orleans Poetry:* "Medusa"; *National Poetry Association College Anthology 1953:* "Song"; *New Orleans Review:* "Heat," "Midas"; *Northwest Review:* "Paranoia," "To Starve a Fever"; *Oxalis:* "Planning Ahead"; *Pegasus:* "Décor"; *Poetry Northwest:* "Advice to the Players"; *PS:* "Regimen"; *Quatrain Digest:* "Thus Let Thy Power"; *Quicksilver:* "Final Poem for a Sequence," "Prose Poems (Group II)"; *The Rolling Coulter:* "Lines from a Postcard"; *Scrap Paper Review:* "To ——— (after Li Shang-Yin)"; *Snake Nation Review:* "Journal Entry"; *South Winter:* "Revisions"; *Southern Review:* "For Donald Justice"; *Tin Wreath:* "Pensées"; *Trident:* "The Caged Cobra"; *Western Humanities Review:* "Epistemological Epigram"; *Wormwood Review:* "Song."

The following poems are reprinted from *Millenary* (New Orleans Poetry Journal Press, 1986): "Assignation," "Heat," *"Luxe, Calme,"* "Medusa," "Midas," "The Summing Up," "A Translation from Memory (Baudelaire)," and "Two Poems for Megan."

All inquiries and permissions should be addressed to the
Publisher, The University of Akron Press, 374B Bierce Library,
Akron, Ohio 44325-1703.

LIBRARY OF CONGRESS CATALOGING-IN-PUBLICATION DATA
Miller, Raeburn, 1934–1990.
The comma after love : selected poems of Raeburn Miller / edited by Donald Justice, Cooper R. Mackin, and Richard D. Olson ; with an introduction by Donald Justice.
p. cm. — (Akron series in poetry)
Includes index.
ISBN 1-884836-03-8 (cloth : ack. paper) : $24.95. ISBN 1-884836-04-6 (paper : alk. paper) : $12.95
I. Justice, Donald Rodney, 1925– . II. Mackin, Cooper R., 1930– . III. Olson, Richard D. (Richard David), 1944– . IV. Title. V. Series.
PS3563.I4198A6 1994
811′.54—dc20 94-32186

Manufactured in the United States of America

FIRST EDITION

Contents

Preface

Four years after his death, Raeburn Miller is a poet whose work is still not well known by the larger audience for poetry in this country, though his friends and students have appreciated it for decades. This lack of recognition can best be explained by his publishing history. Given the diversity of Raeburn Miller's work, it is not surprising that it appeared in dozens of different journals, some of them local publications, and many of them ephemeral, as literary magazines often are. Though he put together seven collections of his poetry, only three of these were published in his lifetime, two as chapbooks and the third as a small press publication. And because he was a prolific writer, a wealth of poems remained in his files when he died. Raeburn's poetry, though not sensationalized or self-pitying enough to be called confessional, always reflected his life. His struggles with love, sexuality, and religion became the themes of many of his poems. This volume of selected poems, drawn from all phases of his long career as a writer, will serve as an introduction to Raeburn Miller for those readers who have not yet had the opportunity to encounter his work.

K. Raeburn Miller (1934–1990) grew up in Austin, Texas. By the time he was in high school, he was already writing poems and submitting them to national publications. At the University of Texas in Austin, where he was elected to Phi Beta Kappa and graduated with highest honors, he pursued his love for the classics and continued to refine his skills as a poet. Selected as a Woodrow Wilson Fellow, Miller entered the Writers Program at the University of Iowa, earning his M.A. in 1958 and his M.F.A. in 1960, the latter under the direction of Donald Justice. After graduation, he accepted a position in the Department of English at the University of New Orleans (then LSUNO) and remained on the faculty until his death in 1990. In his distinguished career there, he also served as chair of the Department of English and as associate dean of the Graduate School.

The purpose of our editorial efforts is twofold: first, to present to the reader a printed selection of Raeburn Miller's finest work; and second, to consolidate all of his poems into a single source. For this volume of selected poems, we were pleased to adopt the title that Raeburn had given to his last unpublished collection,

The Comma After Love. Donald Justice has chosen the poems printed here as representative of the author's most interesting and accomplished work throughout his career. Cooper Mackin and Richard Olson have also assembled on a computer disk all of his published poetry, along with those unpublished poems written since 1960. *The Collected Poems of Raeburn Miller* will be available separately from The University of Akron Press.

In both the selected and the collected works, the poetry has been arranged in the following order: first, poems from the published collections; second, poems from the unpublished collections; third, the published but uncollected poems; and, finally, the unpublished and uncollected poems. Within each category, the poems have been placed in chronological order. The three published volumes are *Fragments from the Greek* (River Road Galleries, 1976), *Sitting in Concord* (University of New Orleans, 1982), and *Millenary* (New Orleans Poetry Journal Press, 1986). The four unpublished volumes are *James Dean Sonnets, To SDL, The Definition of Victory,* and *The Comma After Love.*

We thank UNO archivist Clive Hardy, interlibrary loan librarian Connie L. Phelps, and research assistant William Nores for their invaluable assistance. We also thank all of Raeburn's friends, especially Martha Eckman, Kim Merker, and Elton Glaser, who helped in so many different ways to make this edition a reality. We express our most sincere gratitude to Raeburn's mother, the late Mrs. Peggy Miller, for her very important assistance. Finally, we thank Mary K. Ruetten and Gayle A. Olson for their unfailing support and encouragement.

New Orleans
April 1994

DONALD JUSTICE
COOPER R. MACKIN
RICHARD D. OLSON

Introduction

In terms of literary careers, there are perhaps three or four main types of poets. One conspicuous type seems so much aware of cutting a public figure that the poetry becomes secondary and eventually ceases to matter. Another will by contrast seem hardly aware of a public to be cultivated at all; what matters is just the writing of poems, and doing so may in some cases become a compulsion, secretive perhaps and certainly very private. It is to this second type that Raeburn Miller belongs. He wrote far faster than he published or tried to publish, and he died—a few days short of his fifty-sixth birthday—with a wealth of poems in his files. The feelings a sympathetic reader must have when the work of such writers has come to an end are likely to be a mixture of dismay that so little was seen and known at the time and of pleasure that, after all, so much was accomplished.

Although these poems do not constitute a journal, are not a record of daily life, I think it is fair to say that for much of his life writing poems was for this poet virtually a daily habit. A friend has told me that Miller seems to have composed continuously in his head all day; when he found a moment or two to do so, he would write his poems down. As a consequence they have an air of improvisation, but somewhat studied improvisation, all the same. (So contrary is this to my own practice that I cannot help finding it not only enviable but appealing.)

Miller's poems exhibit a great variety. To me the most interesting of the forms he used can best be described as a sort of chatty meditation, and there exists a large enough number of these to tell us that we are dealing almost with a genre or a type. Of a middle length and written in long lines that owe something—not much perhaps, but something—to Eliot's *Four Quartets,* they are an original contribution.

Among the many shorter pieces, I particularly like his versions of foreign poems, which he treats with a fine careless ease, making them a part of his own sensibility, but always with great respect. Along the way he seems to have tossed off dozens of sonnets, his apparent form of choice. Some, inevitably, contain no more, perhaps, than a line or two of power; but even these stray lines can be dazzling, and it would be a shame to lose them. One story has it that while walking home one afternoon from a class at which the assignment his teacher had given for the week was to write a complete sonnet, Miller had composed five or six sonnets in his head before reaching his own doorstep, a walk of no more than a few blocks. In short, he was a natural poet who found writing a thing he did simply as a part, an important part, of staying alive.

If at times his work lends itself to rhetorical flamboyance and a diction the poet himself associates in one poem with Edna St. Vincent Millay, all of that must be considered in terms of the expansive and unshakably romantic spirit that drives the work and which in the end proves exhilarating. No one could write poems quite like some of these today, but the fact is that they come to us from what is now already the past, though the recent past; and their various styles are aimed faithfully at the timeless and not the topical.

Something R. P. Blackmur long ago had to say of the poems of a recently dead friend can hardly be bettered here: "What had seemed fragmentary, adventitious, disorderly, generally out of bounds, becomes within the bounding lines of death, the very chorus and commentary of the only order of which poetry is capable." The reader of this selection of Raeburn Miller's poetry may well feel initially something of that same sense of the fragmentary and disorderly of which Blackmur speaks, but at some point in going through this life's worth of writing can also count on being rewarded with a second and developing sense of the nature of that life, will find, in all likelihood, that the fragments do cohere, that there is an order that is true to experience and surely worth experiencing. Here, in short, is a life that makes its own sense. I know that such a feeling has grown in me as I attempted to make a choice among the nine hundred or so poems the poet left behind and which have been so carefully and devotedly salvaged by his friends, Richard D. Olson and Cooper R. Mackin, without whose efforts this volume would have been quite impossible.

DONALD JUSTICE

The Comma After Love

A Translation from Memory (Baudelaire)

That servant you were jealous of,
We ought to take her a few flowers—
The dead themselves have heavy sorrows.
I dreamed last night she stood above
Our coupling and would have cried out
From that mouth too far gone for sound.
When you beneath me quicken breath
Let lust unite our thoughts of death,
Let your dark eyes widen and close
To know she still may watch us there
Through those blank sockets where her tears
Last night, all for our sake, arose.

Heat

Northerners warm their hands,
Southerners their rear ends.
Cold hands, you know, warm heart.
But it's down yonder spends

Heat from the heart, attests
To its safety, to its harm.
All lovers go bare-assed.
Though this March day is warm

And I housed close, I take
No chances with desire—
My hands behind my back,
I back up to the fire.

Midas:

Don't say I never warned you
affluence brings with it
environmental pollution—

but keep the gold.
Recently I have spent
my royal highness

counting calories
while a good stereo
plays in the background

semi-classical selections.
Such is the stillness
of a king's poverty.

Go ahead and laugh.
Remember, though,
I once knew gods

and could have fingered you
to gravity forever.
That's done now—

but how you would have gleamed!
I remember those days—
panic, joy,

that heavy wealth.
The lead pencils gold, the lampcord,
my cat a burden on my knees,

its fur still fluffy,
all gold, the *TV Guide,*
the toothbrush bristles

pennies and dimes turned gold,
gold cufflinks real gold,
ping pong balls, Kleenex

crumpled and dropped, ice cream,
storefront glass gone dark,
the mist of gold

blowing off me in a breeze,
such tangible glory!
Certainly I starved,

certainly I mourned—
at a loss to save
my life for such grandeur.

I couldn't manage.
Yet hungry as I was,
I stood a long time

staring down a long time
at those pale sands
where I had washed

my gift away.
Now this rest of me
softens toward death,

empty-handed.
When my father died
he tied a knot,
an intricate legacy

for someone else,
all of Asia.

Not for me—
my ambitions are over,
a memory of brightness

beyond my grasp,
a shimmer, a ripple,
a hearkening of gold.

Medusa:

My halls and garden
are full of statues.
Seeing them one might think

my tastes Hellenistic,
Victorian perhaps,
so accurate the detail,

so consistent the expression
of polite inquiry,
with only occasionally

a shadow like surprise
or the approach of horror.
No, I would have preferred

Brancusi or pre-Columbian,
or better still
something classical,

calm, heroic, unadorned,
naked even.
So many costumes!

When I move among them,
these cold men and women
stare at me.

Stone has the right,
yet I find it strangely hard
to meet their eyes.

Their stillness oppresses
till I long for company,
not this limestone postman,

this iron deer.
It is as if
I were the visitor

and these unyielding lords
had summoned me
in blank condescension

that I should walk the aisles
of their estate
to distract them from weariness.

Two Poems for Megan

I.

You do not know enough to know that weather
Is unpredictable, but has no will of its own,
That when last night was eighteen below zero
No harm was meant. You are so safe, unborn,
That I think of you mostly in terms of self-pity,
Saying, Ah, she must come breathe in the same cankered air
That here rusts my lung, poor innocent, must learn to feel
Her cheeks and forehead tighten numb the first clear night
After snow, only to burn and swell when she arrives home.
And yet I know that where you are, that tangible landscape
Of shelter from the night air and the ubiquitous snows,
Is nowhere for endurance, for a satisfactory translation of
unknowns
Into substantial flakes and encounters, that to remain where
you are
Would be ultimate coldness, your flesh frozen into the cramp
Of sense without the patterning touches of imagination,
That only by unclenching your fist from the warm cordage
And fighting out into alien weather can you hope to achieve
The open porch still beyond passage.
Once here, and despite all our further protests
Of more self-pity that you shall enter the storm
Of death in seldom summer and disaffection,
You must weave your mind toward its perceptible sequence,
Determined to accept your final exposure
As an unsounded reassurance of purpose enough.
And this mindless weather will be your doing, the white snow
Your satisfactory warmth of a larger safety,
And once more you must escape, but this time, kicking free
Of the constricting sky, you will arrive at a wider exile,
And the body you are piecing together now and the
mind's delicate emotions

That you will master in your journey of climate and trouble
Will yield their assertiveness to the breath's luminous demands,
And both the red darkness and the uninformative sky
Will have opened into a true expanse of completeness
    without demarcation
Where blood is Christmas ribbon and the snow falls
For your sake beautifully of its own accord.

II.

One day old and you have already learned
How to glance aside to see your tears' effect
Through glass on our unknown faces. You are stubborn,
I decide, but coy. I go back to your mother.

    Last night I thought a long time about love,
    How any choice is mostly a denial,
    Even holding hands, how there is no way out
    But holding hands—or else going in the kitchen
    To lean your head against the wall a moment,
    Wanting tears, but no outside comfort. And either path
    Is a narrowing of the horizon, a descent.

A couple of times this morning I slipped and called you
My nephew, but then I hadn't seen you cry
With such obvious delight in your own noise
That you had to stop occasionally to chuckle.
I am not likely to forget now you are a woman.
But until you have grown awhile and been hurt,
Your pleasure in tears is too simple. It frightens me.
I go back gladly to your intricate mother.

    Holding hands can be a satisfaction
    Like having the whole apartment to oneself
    Can be a satisfaction. Neither lasts.
    Hands part to light another cigarette
    And beautiful faces in a theatre lobby

Reappear on the refrigerator door
Or over the sprawled pages of a fallen book.

Yet be coy, my dear, and cry. It will get you far,
Though not far enough. But if you learn
Truly skillful tears and to open your eyes,
I know one who once needed such things
And gathered them from air, who is now a mother.

I know what it is like to fear summer
And the lost touch of separated hands
Or to think of getting supper alone at sixty
With an unwashed fork and too much grease, on
a tabletop
Stacked with newspapers and catalogues.
And I know what it is like not to decide,
To wait at night for one trustworthy hint
Past thirty and past forty and past waiting.

You will learn that pearls are lovelier than oysters,
Poems than poets, how to choose stationery,
When to change the subject. And you will be unhappy.
And that is the time to learn another crying,
Silent and dry inside from the long fear
Of knowing and enduring what is yours
Here and no more and inescapable.
That birth-pains should go hard through all Easter
Reminds us, yet is only one granite shiver
From the quarried slope where nothing grows except
The prospect of superior distance, where I have seen
Your mother climbing in the thin sunlight.

To be alone or not be alone
Or not to be. And our choices are made for us.
It is vain to sweat and calculate at night
Looking for theories in the tangled stars;

And whether at last the hands slacken, or never
Never have touched, what is important for our life
Is not the given stone but the long carving
To jewelry sets or garden walls or grave markers.

You were born from two who are in love, who live
Hand in hand, and I, who sulk in a corner
And fidget and complain and eat cake,
Should not instruct you in how and when to cry.
But it does seem certain that pain ultimately
Is the secret, and I would have you grow at last
Beyond mere coyness into knowledge. For that time
I entrust you to your mother and to Our Mother.

And Our Mother of Good Counsel, pray for us.
Empty into our cradled narrow bed
The stubborn light that rushes from your palms
To steal an apple and a rose for love.
Give us our weariness and indecision,
Give us our pain. And help us learn to cry
In coy, genuine tears as winningly
And glance as simply as a one-day girl
Beyond the pane to where all choice is home.

Assignation

I turn the television off
And wait for silence to close in.
Then darkly and alone I fall
To fugitive and cloistered sin.

My toothpaste and deodorant needs—
Consuming passions!—are the same
As for my fellow average men,
Or so the intimate ads proclaim.

But late at night I can break free
To grit my yellow teeth and sweat,
Alone in my one perfect love
Beyond good manners or regret.

Luxe, Calme

Set the prayerwheel where the fresh stream can turn it.
Let your tongue rest from God, let your hands rest.
Love is a burden hour by hour by hour.
Come sink your cool head on my careless breast.

Our eyes have rolled from earth to heaven and closed.
Our throats have swallowed flesh and spat up words.
Our cocks have knelt and spilled life on the ground.
Our minds have dimmed their songs like covered
    birds.

God waits in clockwork, clicking at mere this
That is no love—but let what else be later.
Tomorrow you may save yourself for death.
Let us float now like tired swimmers in water.

The Summing Up

I cannot believe I am unimportant—
a failure, of course,

but such an important failure.
When I say it has been in vain

I speak with such grace,
posturing my splendid vanity.

My sowings wait somewhere,
broadcast, faithful, beyond stone—

some archivist will unfold me
shuddering under my light.

Surely such nothing could not come to nothing.
I buck up,

I start to cook supper,
I look forward to stacking the clean dishes on
    the shelf.

from In Memory of an Actor (I)

Decline is simple, but defeat is hard.
A motor forging forward through dark alleys
I sometimes hear, and thinking of your follies
Beat time to thought and to the motor's word.
Rhythm in all the wisdom I have heard
Teaches that beauty fades before it closes,
Allows a lengthy grief, and then composes
The mind to absence. Quick defeat is hard.

I am not prepared to gather to my heart
This sudden unadulterated vision
Of shattered things that stood so tall before.
My tumbling senses quiver at the hurt—
The stout sound of the towering collision,
The treacherous motor whispering no more.

Tamed with Regret

So much unhappiness without tears.
So much leaning against walls in public places.

So few places to sit down.
So sudden and so familiar, such grief.

Old age becomes recognizable in sorrow,
Spontaneous sorrow, a face in a mirror.

Old age concentrates itself at the joints—
Not in pain, but we think when we move.

Our knees weep now, not our eyes.
Posture has become the difficulty of prayer.

Ash Wednesday

The carnival has come and gone,
I have not told the flesh farewell.
Once I saw truth and turned away.
To turn then is to turn toward hell—

Hell like a Mardi Gras parade
Of maskers tossing cheap nonsense
To outstretched scrambles in the crowd.
Our trinkets buy us no defense.

And no ash burns on my forehead.
My thick flesh celebrates all year
Carnival, carnival, to forget
The endless lent of this despair.

Portal

Better than death, I shall sit here
And think of nothing. So I say.
My gaze drops to the screened front door,
Beyond its frame a summer day.

Tiny coordinates of wire
Mete off decisive boundaries
On the green flourish of the sun.
I too am scored by lines like these.

Such is the nothing of my thought.
And so to death, my thought before—
That time when I must think of all,
As squared whole as a green screen door.

Names and Habitations

Father, I think of Edna St. Vincent Millay
And of how it was all diction with her and still worked,
Of how there are times, walking by a store window
Displaying a fad toy uselessly at forty-eight cents more
Than the drugstore down the street, or realizing suddenly
That the radio I had passively assumed on a shelf somewhere,
Behind the meat counter, perhaps, is actually a transistor model
In the pocket of the young man selecting bread
And he would be puzzled to know I am offended
At his conjoining of our satisfactions—how at these moments
I wish I could do what she did, assimilate beauty
Out of the mere surface of my preoccupations.
There was a time I thought it was the only way
And read nothing but Shakespeare, Hopkins, and the women poets,
But then there was Euripides and no accounting for him
Except in terms of belief distilled to passion,
And when I recognized this, Shakespeare took root,
Was the child too of all the fundamentals I had denied,
Leaving nothing for me to do but begin again.

Yet art that is unequivocally committed to present meanings
Is all the more earthly, and our delicate superstructure
Of faith in beauty for that unmanageable climb
Toward the world of likeness without differentiation
Crumples back to the insignificant level of city streets.
Oh, we keep writing. It has become a habit,
And now that we have learned the secret coordination
Of greatness, we say, it will be just a matter of exercise
To achieve whatever literary reputation we desire.
If we bite our knuckles and believe wholly enough,
We can turn almost with content to the pits of social responsibility
And call them adequate. But to have seen, even in the distance,
A pure form, is to have measured out our frailties

And scarred our inward vision with discontent
For fallen worlds of bargain hunting and football broadcasts.
We search blindly, after motiveless art has proved
Deception, through the deceptions of pleasure and romance,
To the one ascent, rickety and frightening
Through unknown darkness, but a way we always knew
Led to the decisive landscape we longed to reach,
A way we only pretended to ignore
From terror at its demands: the giving up
Of innocent window shopping along with price tags,
Of bread along with radios.
                                        I think of Millay,
Father, and can't help wondering why she
Should have been able to build her pathway so far
Out of idle notions and a bent for the unexpected word.
Why, most disturbing of all, Shakespeare was allowed
To turn an unflinching contemplation of earthly values
Into the shapes of detached art, and then back
To values again, but now crystallized
Into forms as nearly ideal as skywriting.
                                                        I think of Millay,
Sometimes, as I said, with a momentary envy.
But then for relief, Father, I think of Mary
Sitting on the steps listening
While the bread burned in the oven and her sister frowned
Over the account books, of how Martha too,
Though she appeared unworthy, merited your love
By accomplishing her ordered place and is not to be questioned—
Of how even Lazarus achieved your forgiveness when,
Though he had known once before that kiss and its sweet intention,
He fought hard to push away the lips of death.

Journal Entry

The Yale poet from a few years back, or more than that,
Looking like a Dante with narrow hands,
Recited concerning Don Giovanni and Circe,
Remarking later that Snodgrass is too domestic
And that there is a place for minor poets but he is not interested.
Also to be seen, a woman in a red dress
And a gentleman recovering from a broken leg.

Between New Orleans and Baton Rouge
Along the reputedly less interesting highway
There is an interval through palmetto swamps
Where birds whose significant markings I have seen sketched
By two Chaucer scholars independently (and have forgotten)
Wade in their white curves across green water.
I have passed them, driving fast with someone I loved,
And longed for their concentration, for their efficient lines,
For their knowledge of what to grub for in thick swamp water.
I said to them, "Birds! birds!" but they could not hear
To answer with their unflowering of white feathers,
And my love, who thought I had spoken to point them out,
Talked on for miles about having kept pigeons.

So I have heard have heard have heard have heard the story.
The sometime Younger Poet said that hairpins
Could be a shocking thing, that a cup of coffee
Was hard to work into a metrical line.
We all agreed, and down the various circles
Below us all the writhing damned agreed
And the orange knees under the red dress agreed
And I, who drank one beer and came away,
Acknowledge still the truth of his whole story.
As birds and broken legs and love keep truth,

As I, who would give everything I have
To shake out my white feathers now and soar
Above the truth, the foods in filthy water,
Keep honest and with birdsquawks splash to rest.

Paranoia

The wallpaper has turned its back on me.
I unplug my phone to stop it from not ringing.
The memo holders have relaxed off the Frigidaire,
And the compasses have run down like clocks.

Someone hiding in the azalea hums steadily,
Hums all night like a machine underground.
The wisteria next door inhales to speak,
But the wind blows in the opposite direction.

Opposite! The very word is like friendship.
I reach my hand and leave a smudge on the air.
When I make what I make, I drop into cold water
The boiling syrup, but it never hardens.

I have dreamed so well I know what happens next.
They have tampered with my thermostat, but I hide my eyes.
Why must I suffer? What have I done?
I have walked up and down. I confess. Here, take me.

The Lantern

Wherever he was going, he has gone.
I circled block by block and caught his eye
A half a dozen times as I drove by.
Then he was nowhere. I shrugged and searched on.

We can make do for love with anyone
Whose honest falsehood wears the time away.
We live the long hours of our livelong day.
We die and there is nothing to be done.

To say I forego irony is ironic—
All propositions are equivocal.
If truth were simpler, I would simply tell
A tale of what I love, an evening song.
But I seek strangers lightly, like a cynic.
Wherever he was going, he has gone.

Lines from a Postcard

I. *"What Cairo has to tell you is*
survival and relativity."

I had considered verbs, not nouns.
Sentences maybe.
But the oracles speak our own tongue
against us, treacherous as a kiss.
We go to a far country
and find ourselves frightened there
by our own shadow.
In the land of bondage
where the angel of death forever
passes near us, what should we learn
but survival and its law—
not to imagine, not to kill,
not to share the suffering of desire.
I had hoped for one word, not two.
I had hoped to be a stranger, unshod,
slow of speech, to drink blood and part it,
to stand in the center of so many stones,
transient, absolute.

II. *"We frequently go out at 5:30* A.M. *to see a temple."*

To go out before the heat
is to go out before the light.

We are foolish, but we bring batteries.
We make much of time, but we lack roses.

In the shrine of a dead god
our sense of ritual is at a loss.

The postures of theoretical reverence
are to look upward and eastward.

And the day approaches like an enemy.
We go forth as if we were not tired.

Birds are flying early above the dead.
They circle the forsaken temple obediently.

And we whose wanderings are like the lost
find ourselves where we began, having seen everything,

having been turned back from the empty chamber.
We ventured on our pilgrimage from the start

in search of no destination but return,
even as the sun itself ascends towards downfall.

III. *"The volume is astonishing."*

Whether one speaks of the mass of stone
or the mass of space enclosed by stone,
one need not praise to a fat man
the impact of expanse.

When the stone waits in the earth,
a sweep of landscape, of long foundation,
it is one with so much of its nature
that it has no size and no astonishment.

Taken from its place, heaved falsely
by the mind from its endurance,
it thrusts itself into godhead even before its fissures
flake into the likeness of mere god.

And so with blank air.
Left fluid it is full, but fixed
by the pointing finger, the eyes
that determine a straight line,

What was all becomes more,
the container of the uncontained—
the holy whose emptiness
is the surrounded absence of very life.

One is astonished by stone and by what stone holds,
by the nothingness, more durable
than the mind, more durable
than the body that would put on incorruption.

One is astonished and turns away.
Those who stand within this one more vastness,
let them return to their pulse, their purpose, let them make
themselves
infinite by closing their eyes.

IV. *"I will be listening for any other word."*

The word
is always
another word

as the flesh
always is
another, another

dissolution.
We did not catch
what the stranger said.

It was nothing,
she whispered,
turning away.

So that there dwells
among us
no last word.

Our bodies, our
devouring selves,
we have ears to hear

and cannot.
We accept in
place of revelation

the outspoken judgment
of all things, that only
silence is one.

Clouds and Syllables

"How wonderful, and all without understanding a word."

It is June, my dear, here and where you are,
Yet seasons come and go in the post office,
And I, who tend to freckle instead of tan,
Am in and out of the sun, playing with words,
Pretending distance is what keeps us apart.
Words and weather and their various seasons
Were safe, I once believed, to worry about,
Concerns too public, too uncontrollable,
To tamper under the skin with real wanting.

Yet clouds and syllables are what we had,
Hard to understand and intemperate,
And wonder came to us easily and cold
And the ground was too damp to lie on. I sometimes wish
I knew enough to change external things,
Bring the weather around to my way of thinking,
And see if that would help, or polish words
To such proportion and laughter and intaglio
No one could resist reaching out to touch them.
But you are in a foggy place, freshly comforted,
And words flatten like rain against a windshield,
And it is winter in my post office box.

I think I shall go to Texas and visit friends,
Many of whom are literate and many discreet,
Who will understand me if I speak plainly
And answer, There, there, what do we live for anyway
But climate and the affections? It will be warm
This time of year, and wonderful, as they say,—
At night there sometimes, the whole sky is clear

And the eye can see through a great deal, looking upward,
Beyond what is verbal and tempestuous.

1 / 1 / —

"I wanted so much to call you at midnight, even if it would be two o'clock there."

"To seek a myth too actively for too long is no less than a subtle form of self-destruction."

Gentle reader, I charge you with a problem.
I am in Iowa and it is New Year's Day.
And you, though you should prove to be only
My own eyes later sorting hastily through
Unfinished poems, sit in some different attitude
On April grass, perhaps, in Junction, Texas,
Or walk on pebbles under an October sky
Or lie in a hospital bed a long February.
How may I find a compromise with change,
With the Rocky Mountains and the rattling of my alarm clock,
To be able to wish you exactly Happy New Year?

Strangers have strong hands and are easy to love.
We follow the myth. Last night, at two in the morning,
When it was midnight where I wanted to be
And noon in another country, I sat on the floor
Drinking rum punch at a loudmouthed party
And kissing a boy because he was gentle to me
And had strong hands and would remain a stranger.
I wished him, as I wish you, a happy new year.

We follow the myth. It is May Day in Pocatello.
It is autumn in the king's bowels. We are dying, Egypt.
We are dying, Indianapolis, Indiana.
Nancy Kimmel and Paul Revere have the same birthday
But are not the same age, and only the latter is famous
So far. Watching football games on television
Is a subtle form of self-destruction. Happy new year.

I am told ritual can solve any problem,
That "when the saints go marching in" is figurative
Because they are there already, that some bacteria
Can live in boiling sulphuric acid. I know a girl
Eight months old who will someday contemplate suicide
As we all have, and marriage; she is still tiny,
But I watch her clutch and struggle at the bars of her playpen
For exercise, and marvel at how she has grown.
Somewhere the worms crawl in. A week ago
Christ was born and many received Communion.
St. Nicholas came and went. I never envied him
That long ride with so many chances for error.
And here is another year, income tax forms,
Another decade, confetti. May you be happy.

Reader, may you be happy and follow the myth.
May you be gentle and not look back at how
Eating and sleeping are forms of self-destruction.
Two hours ago is now. Last night is now.
And my wristwatch ticks its subtle strangulation
Accusingly, but I am still in love.
The myth is love. The ritual is stillness.
But the time and place of Christ and Santa Claus
Is as hard to understand as all the others.
Reader, I have a telephone call to make,
But first I pray your patience, that I may give you
That greeting, meaningless, human, acceptable
Now and then, where we are, a Happy New Year.

Poem Instead of a Letter

"Love includes the physical of eyes."

I watched a boy on a tricycle as he rode
Beyond the corner of the white garage.
I watched Megan open her red hands
And squeak in sleep, dreaming of colored lights.
I watched her mother in a bright housecoat,
Japanese, left over from the confinement,
Come sleepily through the room and go to eat
A bowl of apricots and three bought cookies.
It is easy to love like that.
Recently a friend
Was hunting an apartment and described
Each one he saw in terms of window space
Until I had to exclaim my sudden horror
At knowing myself opposed to all prospects,
Thinned by views. In every room I have lived
My first concern has been for opaque shades
Without curtains to define what was a window.
For to see out is to escape, and to escape
Is to love too easily and beyond the range
Measured in the tight heart that repeats
"No room, no room!" against each casual invader
Of its difficult round, where love must be kept at a distance
Until it has undergone probing and treachery,
Whatever may be needed to make it humble,
Uncorruptible by power and worthy to rule
An estate so plausible for demagogues
That a profile or gesture has sometimes been enough
To threaten slavery.
Yet windows are necessary
For air and light and believing in the world
That we are not, of apricots and garages.

And love, when we have accepted it by chance,
Measurement, trial, fatigue, and compromise,
Love the hard way, deserves at last its looking,
The seal of its finally uncontested reign,
And short of this remains the neighbor boy,
Never identified, who passed on a tricycle.

My dear, you are eighteen hundred miles away.

The Right Choice

I like to talk about love as if it matters,
To call a life wasted which substitutes
Music or Medicine or Civil Rights
For the proper center of identification,
That dance of call and answer while two, wearily,
Balance themselves by holding on to each other,—
Or, what is perhaps the same love made more acute
By the fists and staircases in childhood dreams,
A saint's marriage in haste to the ideal
Of painful but perpetual ascent.

Little one, what are you dreaming?
I think of the vague Pacific
Threatening you out there;
I think of bars and offices
Where faces come and go,
Of caramel corn and sweaters
To while away money on.
But love, which has its doubts,
Provides its own trust,
Enough for me to believe
In your taste and your defences
And even your thriftiness
So long as you can keep straight
The difference between a city
And an inward destination.

I like to talk about love as the only goal.
But in those pensive moments that follow passion,
When the mind returns coldly to authority
And the body falls away from its insurgence
So tired, then the clock's persistent ticking
Reiterates the propositions of decay,
And all high thoughts of devotion and a durable future

Lie fragile before memories of being alone
Upstairs during thunder, before anticipation
Of unwashed dishes and dust on the rungs of chairs
When tenderness will be answered like an intrusion
And weaknesses once confessed at night in whispers
Eventually sharpen the wit of a party conversation.
Then for a little the mind falters, the center
Sought so long through viewpoints and disorder
Seems the uncertain foothold of another failure,
And one suspects that even the desert saint
Occasionally may see his stigmata scab over
And feel bitter that his duties of perfecting love
Appear to go unnoticed and unjustified,
That God is faithful only in His fashion.

Little one, what are you now?
I think of your face asleep,
Trusting and innocent.
It is early yet, in love.
I still share your belief
In letters and saving money
And a home that can last for good.
But because, even as the young,
We are subject still to dreaming,
For what it's worth I pray
Love is the right choice,
The center poised beyond
Occasional doubts and losses,
The safe place from which
We need not dread to fall.

Storm

Though then we could not have known,
That storm that blew so heavy the night you came
Was the first and deepest of our delayed long winter.
I remember waiting there at three in the morning,
Your bus already two hours overdue,
Among the few soldiers sprawled asleep
Without protection and the few old women.
Occasionally there were rumors that the waiting was fruitless,
But I peered from the window into darkness,
Watching the flakes gather down so thick
They cluttered and varied the blue streetlamp from the corner
And fell like dead weights to the knee-deep earth.
Then gradually, plodding and delicate, the hulk of a bus
Strained silently off of Burlington onto Capitol,
And then it was a bus, not a big truck,
And then it was the right bus with CHICAGO lettered
Above that huge window that had stared so intently
So long at that night's incredible confusion
Of black and white. I went into the snow.
And I remember how your hair whitened as I watched,
How you stood there cursing Iowa in winter
And laughing and saying you had come home.
I think, if I remember right,
I laughed too and denied the bad weather.

Last week I got a note from my mother
Saying she had just found the first bluebonnet.
Here the lawns are still covered grey with old snow
That has fallen repeatedly for so long now,
And settled and darkened and lain dead,
And tonight there is more snow falling, falling,
Beautiful, hateful. I draw my shades.
These days I talk to you occasionally on the telephone
Or when we meet by accident in a bar.

There is a theory, of course, among those people
Who feel they must always know who's to blame,
That our seasons have been so distorted recently
Because the search for new, deadlier weapons
Has left some terrible lack in the whole atmosphere.
I don't know anything about it,
But the idea appeals to me for its simplicity,
Its belief that circumstances can be explained,
And for the sly attraction of any folk magic.
Yet I recall once a long time ago
An old woman making a joke to a soldier
Who was bored and didn't want to hear,
That if the weather kept up as crazy as it had been,
She was ready to believe spring might never come.
Though then I could not have known what I know now,
I remember the fear I felt and the absurdity
At my impulse to accept what she said.

And it is still winter.

I go out in it, cold, dreadful,
I fight the falling of it, I am not ready,
Everywhere I turn,
Endless snow.

Two Fragments toward a Suicide Note

I

I thought today, walking home through the good weather—
Thirty-one degrees by the bank's temperature sign,
But the streets melting even so in the nearing sunlight
For the first time in more than two months,
And I was so happy, walking lightly and smiling,
With two books I had just bought, and planning new poems,
And my love for you like a hand-warmer strapped to my chest,
Everything right between us after such weeks
Of flat lies and distance—I thought today
That this happiness, really, was the mood in which one should
    choose to die.

Not like last Monday night when I came down Linn Street
Early, not much past ten, over packed snow,
Literally stumbling and blubbering
Out of control, loud, all the way home,
And came upstairs crying and lay on the yellow spread,
And no vodka left in the apartment, crying, and finally
Swallowed two Miltowns and six phenobarbs
And lay staring at the snow-lightened night window,
Still not able to sleep, crying, and thought brokenly
All about death. I knew at that worst moment
I would soon be happy again, that killing myself
Could only add to the confusion.
                                        And today I am happy.
I grinned foolishly walking down the street,
But I still know sometime in the run of things
I will probably pity myself enough again
To cry in public. And it seems somehow
That this would be such a right, simple time
To decide, and reconcile my check stubs, and burn my worst poems,
And kiss you just playfully, leaving—

Little one—God—I'm writing—
Don't look at me like that—

II

There are two ways of deciding to kill yourself.
The one is because life doesn't seem worth living,
The other because your life doesn't seem worth living.
(Save that to die—) And the first is what comes to all of us
During adolescence, in study hall, say, in high school,
With the fans turning overhead, when quietly
You admit to yourself that you know you are alone
And the bent faces about you are alone
And no one, not even you, though you may protest
How humble you would be, can give anyone
More of himself than a tone of voice occasionally
And shadows, no more even than your parents give
Who fought all night muffled in the next room;
That it does no good finally to be clever
Or to laugh easily and make everyone say
You are gentle and good-hearted, that even if you were
handsome,
Slender even, you would still be alone.
You sit there, cold, and think of your brother's child,
Seven months done, and know that if you were able
You would see it born dead. But it must save itself
As you must, and you think about how to die.
And the fans turn and the trees beyond the window
Are blurred because you already need glasses.
You retreat then to geometry, pushing away

All you can of that pain for now, and the bell rings,
And you go down to lunch-counter talk in the cafeteria.

That much is common, and there are some, of course,
Who do kill themselves having seen only this.
(Save that to die—) Indeed, when I remember

How early we learn, and how certainly, that life
Means nothing, regrettable, hopeless, it seems absurd
To need to go on and describe a second way
Of choosing suicide, but I think of Weldon Kees
Who sat "in a bar on Tenth Street writing down these lies
In the worst winter of my life," and I think of last December
On one of those quiet days between Christmas and New Year's
When I walked through a public park in clear sunlight
And had my private reasons to look for death.
(Save that to die—) For we can put out of our minds
The general sorrows, the bone tiredness, the bone solitude,
And dwell on sunsets and caresses as though they could last
And dishes and old poems as though they could last
And actually forget mostly to despair.
But a time can come when, knowing perfectly well
There is much beauty in the world, and considerable love,
And clear weather, enough for us to understand
How others might find some reason to go on living,
We are in ourselves defeated,—the career we had worked toward
More or less, shuts suddenly against us like a door,
The poems we had once felt safe to hide in
Go flabby and new ones stick dead half written,
Food even sours in the mouth, home is a trap,
Friendship begins to count money, the church windows crack,
And, above all, love, so light, and so strong,
Leaves us that one face, gently turning away,
With half the words spoken, nothing understood,
Nothing to be done, and pain,
And the future nothing but other losses, meaning less and less,
And all wrong now and for no reason,—
And so, not because we are human, but because we are
    ourselves,
It seems best, and we are tired, not to keep on living.

(Save that to die—) These then are the two ways.
I don't know what good it's done to talk about them.

I am still where I was. And this is the sort of effort
That turns against itself and just stops
Instead of ending, since there is nothing to be said.
Except perhaps this: it is March now.
I have made it through three months since last Christmas.
I shall doubtless live a long, moderately full life
And die of these wounds only in bed in my eighties.
Spring is coming on, my chances perk with the season,
And my love, my foolish one only single love,
Pays attention often when I talk
And cares in a way, enough for my studying and pretending.
And in June I shall go to a better place, where it is warm,
Where the roads are straight for miles and lead places
In order, and the sandstorms are just weather,
And I can breathe and all that—
If only I could stop thinking about it—
What we both want, what I do want—
In June then—I leave my love alone—
Save that to die—

Final Poem for a Sequence

I had an affair with a robot.
—HERMIONE GINGOLD

First there is the end, complicated
By struggle and disbelief, a set jaw
Waged against the telephone, coldly
Biting back simpler words, and eyes held dark
Looking the wrong way nowhere at a party.
But after knowledge that insists and its fixed discipline,
The broader fields of silence and tiredness open,
When we sit calm wondering what to do,
What point in the past, remembered beyond being sad,
We might return to, safely, as a starting point
To begin again, this time dispassionately—
We swear it—the long shudder and swing
Outward toward the darkness of another person.

Say, then, there is a play, French and silly,
About the pangs of disprized love, all in costume.
Take a girl you met last year once to see it
Slightly drunk and laugh in the wrong places
And leave before the neat curtain closes.
In the audience will be strangers you have seen
Outside bookstores, in barbershops, waiting for buses,
Gathered here and shut by darkness for the enactment
Of predictable pathos. Seeing them will bring you
To a mild pity, generalized beyond danger,
And to woodwind concerts later, and a few movies.

Or take, say, a casual friend to dinner
At a better place on the outskirts of town
With late snow falling. From the various tables
Phrases about fireplaces and San Francisco
Will thread loosely about your attention, and occasionally

You will catch at southern voices from another room.
It will be enough to think of richness and travel,
How empty the lives of strangers seem to be
Unless you make up stories for them, the well-served food,
Your abandoned budget.
                                        And yet sometimes in my dreams
It is so black, even yet, and from the blackness
That clicking of steel switches and electric sparks
And the repeated flash of red lights
Coming closer, closing in on me
As I stand helpless, and its steel face
All tubes and fuses, grinding and spinning gears,
The weight of it, all precision and metal,
Moving, crushing, steel thoughts in black wiring,
And those metal lips and metal fingers.

Mnemonics for a Late Spring

I went to look at hunting pants with my partner
And then I went to my psychiatrist.
There were only three pairs left in Sears' basement
And none of them fit. I told him I was glad
Because he wouldn't be able to go out and kill things,
But he answered that he only wouldn't be so warm.
And then my psychiatrist wasted half an hour
Talking about the faculty at Columbia
Before he got around to those same lies
He recites me every Wednesday, that there is hope,
That I am worth the trouble and have won
In the mere waiting—until I could leave his office
Cheerful again, yet knowing full well
There is no hope and all my fluster is loss
And widening loss and I am sick and need help,
Hating myself for being cheered easily.
And then the river to cross, and then the seminar,
And then home to silence and bacon sandwiches.

I bent above the place where the rabbit fell.
Its tracks led there, and those huge boot tracks
Came there and went. A little farther on
The snow was gashed by what was left of the shot.
There was some fur, beginning to blow away,
And three small pits, redder than I had expected
Blood to be. I wasn't much moved,
But my feet were cold and I went back to the car.
As we drove away I remember thinking it strange
That where we had climbed the field, our broken path
Gleamed white in the snow.

And I have dreamed again,
Badly of anger and photography,
Of waste, of death.

Planning Ahead

If I should develop an unusual growth
And after my death they kept it in a bottle on a shelf,
What ought then to be my attitude, looking down at it?

I want to prepare myself now for all eventualities.
I want to think of what I might have to look back on
After death from whatever there is after death.
I can at least arrange that much.

Looking down, or back, on that pickled flesh,
What would be my proper gesture and exclamation?
Let me not seem proud—rather surprised, embarrassed.
Let me say to whoever or whatever may be there to hear,
How interested they seem in it! and Was it really that big?

Ahasuerus:

I am one of those
who will come back
to haunt you.

I know it's hard to believe—
precious few fat men
have that ability,

but just wait.
Five or ten years from now
eating lunch alone

in a booth in a window,
looking out at a street
where two dozen business signs

have worn off their colors,
you'll wonder where I am
who went south somewhere

as casually as a taxi
pulling away from a stoplight.
One day in winter

the grime across the crest
of twice-frozen snow
will shape my initials

and startle you.
It's this trick I manage,
my one distinction:

when I'm there, you call me
a face on a list. But
when I'm gone, I stay.

Poets and Their Bibliographies

Nonumque prematur in annum.
—HORACE

Horace had a lousy vita.
—KATROVAS

Emerson did not remember Days.
Some poems take forever to write.
Some you never find the words for.

There are lines that survive in isolation.
There are whole books praised and never read.
A few poems have had a new life, like Days.

And the garbage dumps of Egypt yield verses,
Or rather scraps of verses among other scraps,
Discarded wrappings that now old men search for.

In a lovers' quarrel the words don't matter much,
But in the fragment of a lost love poem
Ill-sorted phrases keep pace like the days

Passing before us, bringing their various fortunes.
Li Po sat at an inn beside a river
Writing flotsam only the fish would yearn for.

Horace wrote in a dead language.
Horace has published nothing in the past ten years.
Emerson could not remember Days.
Some things you will never find the words for.

To ———
(after Li Shang-yin)

Hard to know, she is hard to part from.
Weathered petals flutter to the west,
Silkworms dangle spent,
Light coagulates in candle sperm.
My mirror clouds with whitening hair
And the round moon is like a gasp.
Her crypt is so close
A mole could bring me word.

Conundrum

When the player in the opposite court
vanishes in a wink,
the ball certainly continues, bounces,
its velocity uninterrupted—
although its unnoticed arc
may carry it beyond recovery,
it is still there.

The question is the racquet—
does that vanish too,
engulfed in the sudden absence,
or does it fall down
clattering and clumsy to the ground,
the relic, the one dead thing?

The Sake of Argument

Let us assume that the simplest version
of the life of Jesus is the true one,
the miracles all miracles, the death
death, the resurrection simply that.
Let us assume incarnation means what it says.

Let us assume our welfare matters to God,
our sins trouble him, our reverence delights.
Let us assume that the appearance of things
is what they are, a flower meant to please,
not some trick for more efficient propagation.

Let us assume that when we die
our soul goes elsewhere to be judged
for every action by standards it can understand,
and that hell burns somewhere below us forever,
and that heaven opens somewhere above us forever.

Advice to the Players

It would not do to write (sigh) after a line,
Or, for modern proprieties, (hysterical laughter),
Or even, as in the funny papers, (sob!).
If the substance is essentially that of good news,
Such stage directions would be gravely improper
Even by implication, even by a faint turning aside
With "Yes, yes, the reward is great, but the abjuring
Is always painful and half-hearted." Such snide hints
That though all shall be well, we may hope the hour postponed
Are finally only one more hidden temptation,
One more vanity, one more pluming of our pride
That after all we have a choice and are making the most of it.
At worst it becomes a way of holding on,
The soldier's parting aria to the fat soprano
While the enemy surely by now has pillaged the country,
The poet's repeated protestations of intending
To decide art is worldly and toss it aside
As soon as this piece is finished and possibly just one more,
The European actor's eighth farewell tour.
                                                            Yet, no matter.
Earth is our home, to be remembered foolishly
Someday, like the slanting peach tree we dangerously climbed
Or the dark hand-worn smells in the saddle house.
If we show less than an angel's crisp bravery
In feeling tender toward it and are slow saying good-bye,
We need only remember that we are still encumbered
With the material manifestations of being created,
That our flesh must eventually reveal its nature
As true earth, to share in the turbulent cycles
Of transmutation, wheeling, caprice, putrescence.
So long as we commit ourselves to saying good-bye,
It is of small importance if we make a production of it,
For in the act itself there will descend
Certain indecisive but urgent assurances

Which will be enough finally to bring us around,
Shepherd us with confidence toward a true taking leave
Accomplished in its moment of ultimately sudden decision
With a joy beyond any fanfare or fluttery regret.

And the choice is to strike a bargain, giving as consideration
All beauty we have sensed here, yes, even hers,
All love of created things, and all the pleasures
That arise from the machinations of body and mind,
And finally body and mind themselves, our only converts,
And, hardest of all, our one distinction, by choice
Abandoning our power to make choices.
In return for such traditional tender we receive
Suffering, our body grown more raw
To darkroom acids, more congested in the wet gaps
Of our lungs and the thin framework of our circulation;
Our mind exhibited to the bewilderment and mockery
Of friends who so obviously wish us well
And are kinder and more gentle than we, that by rights
They ought to know best, but only succeed in leading us
Back toward doubts and dissensions and the throes of
virtue;
Our resolve beset by slashing temptation, in utter obscurity,
Known even as a fool at last only to a few
Incidental strangers and acquaintances.
Then finally we are granted a bare death
Unattended by the dedication of libraries or bequests to
eager cousins,
And burial in the dark beneath a wooden marker
With only the Vision we had put our whole trust in, waiting
Beyond the ravage of pale worms. (Reader, be glad.)

A Red Red Rose

I often think how cheap a love it is
That calls us with its undeniable insistence
To the things of this world, how the immaculate love
Does not constrict itself in the corset of desire
Nor bend under jealous threats repeatedly
Questioning the worth of its fixed commitments, nor fade
From exposure to incompatibility or mental abuse.
The choice is easy enough, and my heart
Accepting the calls and cries of the neuter angels
Wields its silence alone, clumsily,
With praise tendered to its heavy circumstance.

But when, in a dream, someone from adolescence
Who had been all beauty and its close fulfillment
Returns with protestations of having sought
No such betrayal and having remained true
All that time, or when from the crowd after lunch
Waiting for the elevator that will achieve
Their sullen ascension to one more afternoon,
A certain body begins to shimmer and adopt the form
That once we might have envisaged as our true purpose
Beyond virtue and its free choice, had our mind
Been capable of so full an imagination—
Then we look back a moment and ponder
The power still of such irrelevant love
Over our attention, turned with fast assurance
For many days on heaven and our dear intended.

It is natural that we should stand troubled
By these dissensions, guilty and somehow afraid.
But finally, after painful remonstrance
Of our corruptible flesh, after prayer,
After rambling discourse on the significance of temptation,

We come quietly to accept what we have felt
As a part of our duty to this existence,
To be questioned no more than the confusion of our response
Before the El Greco or that sunset once in Texas.
Then, after we have given in and admitted
That sometimes, taken by surprise, at a corner or doorway
Met with a sudden shock of temporal love,
We may acknowledge its satisfactions without yielding
Our ultimate concerns, we come slowly to see
That all love is a degree of one love,
That the dream we had expected to reckon with
At the time of judgment or conceivably of purgation
Was a vision no less from grace than any other,
The pale hands, though unpierced, worthy of reverence
In demanding love. For to love at all
Is to love all; to accept even this beginning
Is to recognize, however feebly, the end
There beyond this pleasure and its renunciation.
And the face yonder tilted up toward the floor marker
To see how far away the elevator has stopped
Which will come to raise us to our appropriate level
Is worthy of what it calls forth in us
As it looks into space and chaos through its holy eyes.

To Starve a Fever

Food is essential and generally pleasant,
Though as children we tended to shy from new dishes
In favor of a conservative hamburger
Or the three pieces of fried chicken our experience
Had learned to trust. But most of us at last,
Excepting, of course, a few mystics and mathematicians,
Have grown to give general approval and social respect
To all fashions of meats, cookies, olives,
Sweet sauce, radishes, pomegranates, and thick cheese,
Even to the unidentifiable hodgepodge
Offered in small Chinese and Turkish restaurants.
It is a pleasure, we say, broad and exciting,
And besides, no one could ever suppose
That eating well is in the least degree improper
Or worldly, for, as everybody understands,
Food is necessary to the preservation of life,
And death, even by starvation, is to be avoided.
It is the same with getting a good night's sleep,
With the judiciously urgent accomplishment of sex,
With the sensuous exhilaration of opening a checkbook,
With the poem a friend quoted piecemeal on a bus
Or the oboe music Andrew was overheard whistling—
In short, with all the fancy manifestations
Of our spatial and temporary vanities;
For, we are assured by the evidence of things seen,
And in spite of childhood misgivings looking sideways,
These are the attainments that make life worthwhile,
Possible even—the comforts without which
We should suffer crucial agonies and die helpless.

But occasionally, most often at night when sleep
Somehow will not do more than float thinly
Through the corridors outside, there comes to us

A whim—we like to term it a realization—
That, after all, our meticulous ease, the artifice
Of comforts and beauties that break or get lost,
Cannot truly shield us from the shocking
Ferocity of change, from uncertain and haphazard failures,
Nor teach us any strong safeguard against Death,
Not even a way to assume satisfaction
With the futility of his unrealized distances
And the inexorable decomposition of our costly flesh.
Whether it is the inspiration of genuine grace
That calls up such imaginings, or whether
We should blame cucumbers in the salad at supper
Or the simple lying awake too long
Or the unacknowledged frustration of encroaching impotency
Or the overdraft notice, surely a mistake,
Or the blunt phonograph needle already played
Far beyond its rightful service—the true cause
Of such doubts is not for our speculation.
Whatever the reason, such doubts come,
Troubling, sifting, and distorting our allegiances,
As the wind across a desert may veer in the night
To leave the sand rippled in another direction,
Deceiving the conformities of light and shadow at dawn
To opposite patterns and more complex cross-purposes.

St. Catherine, pray for my soul.
                                        You remember,
I think, how importunate and conclusive sometimes seem
The domestic affections and the cultural commitments
That weight us down steadily to earth.
Send us the proper visions of our consummated extremes—
Whether through angelic visitation or through providing
Cucumber salad and worn phonograph needles
Is of no importance. I leave all that to you,
You who consumed night in virginal devotions,
Day in the perfecting of your poverty,

For whom no earthly artist in delicate gold
Could fashion any inducement to reject
That bauble which manifested its splendors unseen,
You whose only nourishment was your husband's flesh,
The red token of what suffices, the bread of the angels.

Love Poem

The likeness between the pagan gods of Greece
and their hearty Roman counterparts
is never exact, but usually clear—
a shift of emphasis, of personality,
like lost friends at a high school reunion,
gesture and tone of voice suddenly unchanged.

But not the gods of love—Amor and Eros
are at best hard brothers, like Cain and Abel:
the one cold, the other cool,
the one quick-eyed, the other earnest.
I have lifted my hands before their opposite altars
and prayed to each for deliverance from the other.

And once in a bright sky, above a pale landscape,
I saw a host of putti rolling in child's play.
I myself, with my own eyes.
Although they looked as cunning as kittens,
I was frightened that they should be revealed to me.
I wondered whether God had mistaken them for angels.

On the Success of Former Students

As many words as the Eskimos need for snow
I need for jealousy, or for the stations between
that kind of reaction and the reactions of pride,
an irregular range that includes disbelief and fear.

When I recite the Apostles' Creed by rote
I feel something, but not doubt or fear.
I have most trouble with the forgiveness of sins.
And I fudge a little on the Holy Catholic Church.

But I do believe in the resurrection of the body
simply, in spite of this body, of all evidence.
And I believe as simply that the success of others
will be changed utterly, will put on incorruption.

I believe that my own failures will rise from the dead,
in petulance, in awe, in hope, in exasperation, in mercy.

After Wang Wei

I mix a last drink and ask about your choice.
You seem as uncertain as you are determined.

"It was turbulence that made the choice, not I.
To the south, they say, the mountains themselves are calm.

You must not ask where I am going.
It is where there are white clouds overhead."

Thus Let Thy Power

Beauty walks in stride with death
Death is Beauty's mother
We who have known one of them
Need not fear the other.

Décor

I shall put roses on my ceiling for those who yet look up,
But I shall also polish my floors for those content with blurred reflections.

Rationale of Dissipation

So what if I *should* die at last with gout?
There will be twelve good feet to carry me out.

Letter Found in a Refrigerator

Dear Father, Come home. The toothpaste won't hold anymore,
And the cats spend all their time in the chandelier.
What is worse, there is no sign of either Henry.
The neighbors all try to blame the hurricane,
But I for one lay it to drink. We have plenty of salt,
But the sugar is turning blue, and the more I sun it,
The thinner it gets. I am doing a sampler for you
With the motto, "I would make a good husband,"
But the polka dots keep falling off. On top of everything,
I have actors all over my hands, and the more I wash them,
The worse they stink. In short, as you can see,
The whole damn mess is brisk and flavorful.
So please try to come home. Your friend, (unsigned.)

Epistemological Epigram

The biggest things must be
At last the least of me.
The only total sky
Is closed within my eye.

Prose Poems

Group I

I. My uncle always interrupted others and insulted women by assuming they remembered the First World War. He was an accident, my favorite uncle, that befell only those who were fully insured. A premium is small, but even so. I am not quite certain any longer that he was a nice man.

II. The wallpaper was called a dove pattern, so she told everyone that the chickens on it were turtledoves. Even she could not pretend the turkey was, but the chickens were just abstract enough. When he showed her the real doves, tiny in flight above the empty cages, she was convinced, but unhappy. I wanted them to be the white ones, she cried, her sorrow central to her choice, to her propriety.

Why, just look at those saddles, another woman said disdainfully. She meant the wings.

III. I saw him on a corner with others and hurried on, knowing that should the traffic, bad there, do what it could so easily do, it was more fitting that someone else carry him to a hospital or a mortician, for he and I never talked much about any of the serious matters beyond our own power to act, and he would not understand why saying hello on a street corner should not satisfy me for a good goodby.

IV. Oh yes, there are ghosts, but only in the street. I see them, thin and crucial, not because they were there once but because they are there now. And the colors are green and blue on the street now, though where you are it may not be the same. Coming into the apartment, I find the angels no longer about, their wings stuffed down into the wastebasket, the curtains no longer busy with their hiding and flight. I have thought that the ghosts may be the angels, only outside now and without wings, though the ghosts say other things and are visible. And inside, the colors as well that once were so gaudy are shaded, undone, changed perhaps outside to that mere green and blue, as it may be even where you are. I don't need much, you know, and inside would be a good riddance, if I could be sure it was lost, not changed.

Little one, how you carry on.

V. This is the third time this summer that I have been hurt because a woman I did not love loved someone else. Mushrooms are what they sell at the store. Toadstools are all the rest.

VI. Well, if it comes to that let there be dissension between the seeds if it will make you feel any better. All that matters is that we have been honest as often as we said we loved each other so often so many times.

VII. She has learned to walk, but not well yet, especially on such a rug. Today as she felt herself losing balance and clutched at the arm of the typing table, it slipped from its support and came down, delaying her fall only long enough for her to know she was helpless, to feel in her tilting vision how it was too late. And she cried harder than after far more painful tumbles.

I have thought a lot recently about death.

VIII. Where I grew up we spoke of jumping from the University tower, and here we speak of throwing ourselves into the Iowa River, and where you are, it is always leaping from the Bay Bridge. Even Peru, Nebraska, has its traditional water tank.

But I am lazy and like to lie down. I hang up the phone now and turn toward the wall, unhappy, with neither tears nor prayer. You are not alone, I can ignore your bridge a while longer. I, less dashing, you know, once saved up 460 sleeping pills.

I had fallen before, in love.

IX. (for JRD)

I still do believe in love. But many pedestrians are killed every year, although they had the right of way.

Group II

I. The sick mind manifested in fish scales and loud issues draws skin over its outward slashes and rots toward the center to make Iowa in the North. I wish I could go home where madness is what everyone is willing to fortify with active nonchalance and smells so pleasant in the open like a brown cake still warm from the oven. The sun shines.

II. She came from behind the chimney saying what does it all mean with her arms flung out and an ungraceful walk. It is perhaps a good thing that people get hurt and go away, but I for one desire, more than I care to say, just once to be there when everything visible slips a little to the left and the mind of an onlooker must henceforward wince at the idea of sequence and get drunk and imitate the way she threw out her thin arms and cry and go away.

III. I like to talk of killing myself because when it turns warm and the snow melts I am not at all disturbed. I once walked on a frozen river but had a hard time getting back up the bank and was so happy, so moved.

Convertible Invocations

O the jewel in the lotus. O
That feeling when you are really doing eighty,
But it seems as if you're going ever so slow.
O Santa Claus. O halibut. O the weighty
Problem of where to bury your secretary
When you have ink all over your hands, but have to hurry.
O the way your eyes close and your stomach is heavy
When beyond the shadow of a doubt you know
There is no more hot water. O jonquils. O the worry
Of feeling holier-than-thou when you are in a bevy
Of ministerial students on their spring outing.
O ice cream. O ice cream and vodka. O the coarse shouting
Of the suspiciously blue woman in the vision.
O the blunt instrument never handy when with indecision
A friend makes a point of saying you look well
But purses his lips to show you he is doubting.
O Capri. O mother-love. O hell.

On Millay's Translations of Baudelaire

I. Failures

Lady, these doings smell of lavender.
Go home and wear an apron and be still,
Polishing pots and sonnets to your will.
Let evil be its own interpreter.
Such lace as you have snarled about us here
Clutters the form you struggled to reveal,
Yet loosely fretted, cannot well conceal
Old vices through its openwork veneer.

A mole is blinder with the falcon's eye.
Waves are the ocean's wild attempt to climb.
But the tall wing is nimbler in the sky,
And the wide sea will crush all peaks in time.
My sweet, sufficient singer, need you try
To garland evil in such chastened rhyme?

II. Devices

The hangman's knot is native to the lung
That would stretch out its own taut noose one foot a while.
Who dreams his clever pleading can beguile
Fixed strands of air is looking to be hung.

The golden cells locked in their hive of bone
Must ripen singly by proportioned style.
Robbing the comb past season will defile
Honey for even your accomplished tongue.

Mellifluous demands require a setting
Of received bounds to hold their sweet secure;
Denying these you made our verdict sure.
With covered head the judge begins to quote
That staple sentence you are past regretting
And asks time's grace on your contorted throat.

III. Responsibility

From dreams, or from the gravel in the pan,
Or from the country you remind me of?
We curse the chisel when we must absolve
Marble which art corrupted into sand.
Yet if the shaft splinters in the hand,
Know that the mountain's passion, seeking birth,
Has often heaved and shuddered through the earth,
Wounding the long foundations of the land.

In dreams, as well, responsibilities
End. There is little worth in gold alone
Untroubled by the mud's thick rivalries.
And shores away keep semblances their own.
So let him call to judgment here who sees
The sculptor cloven by the faulted stone.

Scraps

We threw our watermelon rinds
Into the hen house with a yell.
Their crispness green against the sun,
They bumped and skidded as they fell.

Then when the beaks had pecked them dry,
They withered yellow and were gone.
The puling-minded chickens gaped,
Batted their wings, and rumpled on.

The egg is sturdier than the seed.
What have we proved who proved it so?
Between our picnic and the night
We fold a tablecloth and go.

The Caged Cobra

(after Rilke)

Not doubtful shades beyond, but this screen wire
Fixes a usual distance for his eye.
Weary of search, he reckons everywhere
To be the reaches of his checkered sky.

The rhythmic flick of his exploring tongue
Can probe his utmost universe, until
He stuns in the embraces of his strong
Lithe coils the workings of almighty Will.

But when his lidless eye unwittingly
Falls on some truth those farther shapes impart,
The sight shudders through him soundlessly
And clots in his cold, beating heart.

Regimen

I eat cheese dips and pie
And vitamin pills. I talk
Long hours with casual friends.
Occasionally I walk

A block or so. I teach
Half-truths by rote. At night
I wait up through the news.
And now and then I write.

My subject, tragedy.
My form, deliberate verse.
My end, a sort of prayer
Against this vacant curse.

Revisions

Shall we take rancid butter for a sign?
I doubt the iceman is a witch, but how
Shall we distinguish butter from the cow
If meddlers still change water into wine?
Dante beheld his Lady's features shine
Upon a mountain top, but in an hour
The allegory turned the vision sour.
Is Paradise above the timberline?

My Father, if you say so, I'll get by
On blinky milk and third-rate science fiction—
I only ask a clarified design.
For now your will's in pieces, and my eye
Strives to match meaning from these contradictions:
Your wicked generation seeks a sign.

For a Saint

> *To protect statues against birds' droppings, disks were affixed to their heads, the probable origin of the nimbus of the saints in Christian art.*
>
> —OWEN

Use hard money to buy your bread.
Wear a thimble when you mend your clothes.
Never believe this neon round your head
Offers the safety neighbors may suppose.

Your blood will prick through as quick as any.
You know rips and hungers and neighbors' words
And worry about next week's money
And overhead the sinister flight of birds.

Dispositions

The good thief lingered and they broke his bones.
He wrenched askew alongside his dead Lord,
True in those last contortions to the word
Wrung from him in a testament of groans.
Below him Romans, their priesthood unknown,
While waiting for the dead to die, grew bored,
Took God's homespun disguise for their reward,
And flustered ivory counters on the stones.

The good thief and the soldiers were forgiven,
He for late faith, they for their ignorance:
So stretch the circumstantial routes to heaven
Where minds grow whole and risen limbs knit well.
The left-hand thief, who mangled his one chance,
Grubs on crushed thighbones back and forth through hell.

For Donald Justice

(after Li Po)

I met you in an overcoat
in the Corn Belt in August.
Why are you so scrawny?
Been living on poetry?

A Curse from Propertius

The gods must grant me this one prayer
Who kept long faith and slept alone:
Rocking on your soft breast tonight
Let your new lover turn to stone.

When workmen come to cart away
The obscene statue from your bed,
Let them slip and knock its hard-on off
And chip the damp curls from its head.

Beyond some rutted country slope
Then let that banged-up artwork stand,
As far and lost as your false heart,
To scare the birds from pasture land.

Pensées

They hang from the rafters like heavy clouds,
They are long, they make sense—

Whatever order they may have
It is solemn and final,

They are dead, they are the dead.
My hands are tied, says the bacon.

My knuckles are white, says the bat.
And from the distant scaffold it is the dead eyes,

It is the dripping water,
It is the dripping stone.

My mind is hanging, my mind hangs,
I am a dead weight,

The arc of my dangling marks no time.

Gulf Breeze

(after Mallarmé)

The flesh is sad, the books, alas, all read.
To get away somewhere! I dream of birds
Drunken in a strange splash of wave on sky.
No inland vistas can catch back my heart
Whose beating plunges seaward through the night,
Nor the perspectives of my lamp
Across white paper armed with innocence,
Nor the tableau of any girl and her child.
I must set forth! Tall ship, make bold your rigging—
Lift anchor toward some world I have not known.

My emptiness, long hopeless for life here,
Believes I still somehow could wave good-bye,
The steady masts somehow urge on the storms
To sweep me above wrecks in a vast wind
Lost and alive, lost from the stifling land—
And oh, my pulse, recite the sailors' chant!

Peptides

Impelled by how unjustified it is
when joy arrives, we must accept at last
chemical imbalance as its source,
and yet joy, oh, we do embrace its
coming, we do take it personally,
we do spread our arms, our
weak, slow, uncomprehending arms.

Q.E.D.

Let me begin by saying I am tired.
I have no poems to write. I write no poems.
I am not writing very much these days.
The muse does not descend. I am not writing.
Today is the twenty-third of February.
I find that I have nothing left to say.
Yesterday was the twenty-second of February.
It takes a special mood to write a poem.
I haven't felt like poems recently.
Tomorrow will be the twenty-fourth of February.
I find I now read literary criticism
At night in bed before I get to sleep.
I say my day's work deadens me for writing.
I haven't written for a long time now.
I call myself a slave to television.
I say I watch TV instead of writing.
There seem no poems left for me to write,
So that I don't write poems the way I used to.
I don't write poems like that anymore.
Today I saw a pear tree. It is spring.
If I remember right, last month was winter.
Summer at length will transpire, I suppose.
I used to watch and turn aside and write.
I used to fend off seasons from the world.
But pear trees cannot lie about the season.
I write no poems. I am growing old.
I write no poems. And food and architecture
And eyes in photographs—it leaves me tired.
I have no poems to write. I write no poems.

Triptych

I know a former orphan
Whose lovers live alone.
His kisses fall at random,
But his toothbrush is his own.

I know a lace-thinned lady
Whose skin's like watered silk.
Her love affairs end early
With lemon served, or milk.

I know two beefy poets
Who belch and go to bed
In Bowling Green, Ohio,
Where angels fear to tread.

Epitaph

(after the Greek)

I who am dead beneath this stone
Slept my long sixty years alone,
A fate my father should have known.

A Soliloquy for Seraphia

"How can we know. . . ."

Sgt. Barry Sadler is singing "The Green Berets."
Tuesday morning I was driving down this same street
With the radio playing at about this same time
While Sgt. Barry Sadler was singing "The Green Berets,"
And I began to cry and kept crying the rest of the way.
This morning, driving down this same street,
When he began, I reached to change stations
But pushed my hand away as if it were not my hand.
He is singing—and again now I am starting to cry.

That my daughter wakes me with an earache or nightmares,
That my body chides me to enclose another child,
That executives never show they are suffering,
That students don't read, that students read without listening,
That students readily sit in judgment on Shelley,
That men in jungles ten thousand miles away
Dance and dance and dance: it is all one.
I drive without paying attention, crying for the dancers.
For Sgt. Barry Sadler singing "The Green Berets."

And time falls down. My hand is not my own.
My tears roll down from eyes that are not my own.
The dance in time, the dance incarnate,
The dancer, my daughter sitting beside water,
The distance, the singing, the still bodies.
Straining to listen for distinctions. The keeping time of tears.

Song

An hour past Sunday
Of a night on the town
With a parking-lot hustler
To blow the man down.

A name or a number
Is lesson too much:
Knowledge is power
And power corrupts.

Who is my neighbor?
Neighbor I've none.
Let all true lovers
Lie down alone.

Depression

The sky's a lid and the eyelid a sky.
Hustlers at bus stops stand in their underwear.
To an Asian king I cannot recognize
I make obeisance and stumble.

The sky's a dutch oven and the heart leftovers.
Beneath the smooth bedspread the sheets are wrinkled.
I measured the lumber needed for the new scaffold,
But afterwards I could not balance my check stubs.

The sky is a stopped sink, my mouth is no friend.
My mouth churns with rubber and lye.
God will trick me by existing if I lift my hand.
I will call my own bluff. I will keep on.

Expectancy

As if the way could end,
as if the beginning could end,
he measured himself in money worries.

He jogged, he was a sick man,
he told himself stories,
he longed so for a conclusion.

But that stain where the roof leaks,
that's how we all last,
always damp or always to seem so,

unique, unwelcome,
as forever as a jug's lovers.
Whatever he walked out on

got better, he heard.
He wanted that on his stone.
He forgot to say so.

He wandered in a circle, like the lost.
He lived on.

Philistia

I have written so much
and so much has meaning
only to me and so
much to no one.

So much has no life,
no completion,
gaps like shallow rivers
a mile wide.

To stay home is to come home.
It is as well
to fail. There is security
in the never broken hive.

If a tree falls so far from us
that only the bees hear,
does its trunk of honey
have a taste?

So much remains
to be done, so much
lies in remains, I
go to sleep surrounded.

A sense of accomplishment
drips from the brow of
Adam, who cannot concentrate
on his curse.

And what should the world be
but lost? Let it stay lost.
The barren somehow bear most,
I have written without

paradox. Even if at last I must
go forth to blind labor,
in my violence I cry out
still: I am the eater

whose putrid side
swarms with meat, I
am strong for now in my
own sweetness.

As You Say

Languages can exist without yes and no.
So many words are essentially meaningless.
What does foot mean or tulip or hair?
(How should a young philosopher talk of hair?)
Not to mention contend or dissolute.

Is it for meaning after all that we thirst?
That we kick the rock with our staff to bring forth
The water of God's elaborate disapproval?
The meanings of water that would speak God's approval?
Elijah on Carmel remembered Noah.

And yes and no go in by two and two.
Once bulbs were smuggled abroad at great price,
This species double or that species black:
Nobody denies a flower its due, however
Rare, erotic, unscented, given to gossip.

We nod affirmatively and fall asleep,
And silence gives consent, say the morticians.
Yet the dead return, shuddering, uncompliant,
And the stars, oh, they struggle and fly apart—
Oh, what is there to say, they are meaningless.

An Eventual Elegy

I took notes at your graveside—for what?
The notes remember a wishing well nearby.
It seems unreasonable, but I guess so.
Maybe I threw a coin in. The notes don't say.

How many years are you dead now? Almost
twenty?
More than twenty, I suppose. Time flies—
Flies in circles, like a vulture, above where
Something concluded, something else moved
on.

You are my memory that has left things out,
This scrap of notebook paper, already brittle,
This page of verse now, this late, getting
written,
That grave, those plaques, that artificial well.

I mock myself as knowing and feeling nothing.
If I should make a wish tonight, I would call
Pale nymphs to lavish flowers upon your grave
Whose deep roots draw untainted aquifers.

Such the non-wish of a penniless man.
My memory may be false, self-serving,
infrequent,
But I can offer you what there is of it,
That I still stand at your grave, that I wish you
well.

Recalling Cottonwoods

A hundred reasons I was not a Texan,
however much I tried to be and thought I was,
but I took no precautions against ridicule.

I spoke my mother's middle-American English.
I behaved as one neither rich nor poor, nor both.
Detached, self-conscious, I was no Texan.

I loved the stars, I loved roadside flowers,
I loved the names of animals and towns,
the way any lover invites ridicule,

yet I loved with an outsider's speculative view,
framed by the assumptions of a different West.
Lover or loser, I was no Texan.

And I left with little regret and went away
nowhere much though certainly elsewhere,
having taken no precautions against ridicule.

There is some part of me, dry as a bone,
scared as a rabbit, still some place down home.
A hundred reasons I am not a Texan,
but I take no precautions against ridicule.

High Five

A father and small son
slap hands, one arm
reaching up, one down,

and years later that son
will know the gesture
was otherwise in the

mind of both, both
arms raised, and with his
later friends will reenact

what he understood,
not what he did. It is
that way with fathers

and sons. And Isaac grew
to lift his hand, whose
father had lowered his.

News Photo

Nature is the opposite of the soul.
—EMERSON

The electron microscope shows an AIDS virus
"budding" from the side of a white blood cell.

Metaphor too when we speak of eddying stars—
hair that flows, or rhetoric, even pity.

But there is no figure of speech at work
in the blood stream or the stream of consciousness.

And as falls are unaware of the mists they scatter,
splashed blood keeps no memory of the life that colored it.

****

A soul takes its figure from its own nature,
like a flower, as we say, or like flowering pestilence,

like a spray of negatively charged particles
sending vision deeper into nothingness,

like itself, like the soul of which it is a part,
like a smooth stone over which a clear stream rushes.

Rewriting Another's Draft

Even if one makes no attempt to sound like someone else,
one sounds like someone else—the sentences
seem to be spoken from a face on a poster
or from one carved in shallow relief on a stone wall.

Nor is prayer ever entirely our own.
The inner self is also another for whom we speak,
needs help, has no style, no facility.

Language is difficult differently from thought.
Voices from another room speak in ominous
incoherencies, and the secret collaborator
succeeds by being faithful only to himself,
a traitor who prospers.

The Nudist in Drag

His tailor wrote beside his measurements
"Shaped like a woman," and a friend
newly paroled assured him that in prison
he would never want for cigarettes.

He was old enough to abide in the discomfort
of his proportions, even if not lightly.
Year by gradual year his body became
less important as a friend or as an enemy.

And he remembered that nameless young man
in loose attire who fled and left behind
the linen cloth and his dignity—left, indeed,
his word to one who also had been made flesh.

On Teaching Another's Keats Assignments

"Sweet little red feet! why would you die?"

I suppose she assigned the sonnet on Lord Byron
To show them how bad the early Keats could be.
But wasn't one enough? Why did she go on
With "I Stood Tiptoe Upon a Little Hill"
And "Sleep and Poetry" and a dozen others?
She must have had something better to say than I have.

Keats died a lot younger than she is dying.
Those last bad months when he was too far gone
To write—what were the words like in his head?
Noiseless noises or And little town?
Beamily or perilous? or perhaps he heard
The voices of others gathering in the skies.

I can make do, can teach equally well
The handful of masterpieces and the claptrap,
I know a thing or two about humming and faking it.
The students will be bravely through it all,
Life, faery land, metrical variations, death.

And her death will not come until later,
When the semester is over and the students
Have finished Keats and got on with their lives,
When I have lifted these odd poems back to their shelf
And come to myself upon the cold hill's side.

The Shape of Things

Don't cry—not a big round tear—any kind but that.
—to her granddaughter

The infant shares her tears. We tell her not to.
How beauteous is the morning. She wakes us crying.
And once I woke in the middle of the night
To hear a boy jabber his brother's name
And cry, to hear another abandoned one
Protest "I can't understand it" sleepily,
"Why won't she let me meet her—in public, in a bar?
It's not as if I meant to ask anything,"
And cry. That was the middle of the night.
I can't remember what the tears looked like.

(Child, I will tell you how it is with us
Who wake in the morning and are seldom answered:
We eat too much. We go to bed with strangers.
We have political responsibilities
And pray on occasion and keep the bathroom door shut
And draw aesthetic judgments about the shape of things.
We repeat turns of phrase. When we are afraid,
We make toys out of our friends' failures.
And when, against our training, we are overcome,
We wipe our eyes quickly and turn aside
Embarrassed, selfish.)
And in the mortuary
The assistant came from the back room in a stained apron
To greet the relatives with a proper concern
Short of tears. I had a friend who worked there
Answering the telephone with the easy number
When it rang in the night.
And once, having given up
Art, you know, and love, and the grand ambitions,

I went back to the Texas coast and sat for a time
On random driftwood, poking at clam shells and sand dollars,
While the bloodshot heavens widened over me
And the water rolled at my feet like a tear.

Vitals

"Hurt them till it helps"

One worries about money
with one's mother in a home,
the car likewise dying, the stock market
weighed down by self-pity.

And one holds one's heart in one's hands
curiously, like a thoracic surgeon
who, after so many years of doing it all,
still at times feels helpless and mysterious.

There are so few cures and they come at such cost.
Who operates on himself has a fool for a patient—
is forced by circumstances to make house calls
but keeps the bad news from himself.

These are my hands certainly, and this may be my heart.
The doughty chambers are still at work
even in my hand, disconnected, out of whack.
They are gradually transforming themselves into something else,

something empty, smooth, something like a safe
found open, or like the gigantic magazine
of a revolver in a dream, falling through water,
its ability to kill becoming an ability to die.

Some Sums

1.
He will die who
eats mushrooms
for their beauty.

2.
Leave a space between the words
as if you were telling the truth.

3.
Fifty years still
reforming the language
as a first step—

4.
He came from South Dakota
and thought the river mist
was air pollution
as it may have been.

5.
The modern suicide
inexperienced at letters
leaves a phone call.

6.
as slowly
as a star

7.
He dispersed the crowd
and found across the neutral ground
a scattering of phrases.

8.
The produce stalls display
black grapes in plastic,
like fixed rapids in that
last river.

9.
At the fair the
man who swallowed swords
also spat them up.

10.
reverence without referents

11.
uphill all the
way walking a
bicycle

12.
like Satan
stupidly good
momentarily

13.
the taste of canned vegetables,
of the afterlife

14.
If you stop that noise,
I will tell you a story—
I will explain in detail
why they call Mimi Buttercup
and Buttercup Mimi.

15.
old age, choosing
vanilla ice cream

16.

better chastity than contraception
better contraception than abortion
better abortion than pestilence
better pestilence than starvation
better starvation than mayhem
but take what you can get

17.

Like one blackmailed,
he pays the bill from
the nursing home,
thinking of other
ways out.

18.

here and
there, here
and there,
here and
there there

19.

If I had something else
what I have would be
what I wanted.

20.

The lawn takes
those who care for it
for enemies.

21.

He stood at
the mountain top
and wanted out.

22.
As he crossed the
dark garden his
flashlight struck
a stone Priapus,
that sun god—

23.
One picks a hook
the appropriate size
for fish as yet
only imagined.

24.
No spell transforms
random numbers into
random words.

25.
I'm going out to spread manure.
You come too.

26.
Be happy
he never said
to judge the fruit
by its tree.

27.
The three have only one eye,
Depression, Anger, Fatigue.
It's Fatigue cuts the thread.

28.
We imagine
the Child Jesus
wondering, delighted,
different from the man.

29.
The criminal hides from
retribution beside
the hospital bed.

30.
At last he had
made a home of his
unknown whereabouts.

31.
Old age—
suicide has
less point.

32.
We—he was interrupted
after one word, started
again, and finished—I

33.
Though lost
the souls in hell
know where they are.

34.
The "secret hero," yes
each poem has one,
each effort, each
looking at the sun.

35.
The cameo
fills a whole room
of the doll's house.

Index of Titles and First Lines

ABOUT THE AUTHOR

RAEBURN MILLER was born in 1934 in Austin, Texas. He completed a B.A. at the University of Texas and an M.A. and M.F.A. at the University of Iowa, where he studied with Donald Justice. Miller taught in the Department of English at the University of New Orleans from 1960 until his death in 1990. Two chapbooks and one full-length collection of poems, *Millenary,* were published during his lifetime. *The Collected Poetry of Raeburn Miller* will be available in a special edition on computer disk from The University of Akron Press.

ABOUT THE EDITORS

DONALD JUSTICE, whose first book, *The Summer Anniversaries,* was the Lamont Poetry Selection for 1959, and whose *Selected Poems* won the Pulitzer Prize in 1980, taught at a number of universities, including the University of California at Irvine, the University of Iowa, where Raeburn Miller was his student, and the University of Florida. Now retired from teaching, Mr. Justice lives in Iowa City, where he continues to write poetry.

COOPER R. MACKIN, a Milton scholar who earned his Ph.D. at Rice University, was for many years a colleague of Raeburn Miller at the University of New Orleans, where since 1990 he has been Chancellor Emeritus and Professor Emeritus of English.

RICHARD D. OLSON is Research Professor of Psychology at the University of New Orleans and the author of more than 80 papers in psychology. A long-time friend of Raeburn Miller, Professor Olson is executor of the Miller estate.

ABOUT THE BOOK

The Comma After Love was designed and typeset on a Macintosh in Quark XPress by Kachergis Book Design of Pittsboro, North Carolina. The typeface, Adobe Garamond, was designed by Robert Slimbach, and based on a typeface designed by the sixteenth-century printer, publisher, and type designer Claude Garamond. Adobe Garamond was the first Adobe Originals typeface.

The Comma After Love was printed on sixty-pound Glatfelter Supple Opaque and bound by Thomson-Shore of Dexter, Michigan.